the book

thai

cookbook

by Chef Tummanoon Punchun

Delicious recipes like Tom Yam Soup,
Pad Thai and Roast Duck in Red Curry that embody
the best of Thai cuisine.

PERIPLUS

The Boathouse Restaurant and Culinary Workshop

Of the nearly 20 beaches and small coves strung like pearls along the western coast of Phuket, among the most alluring is Kata near the southern end of the island. M.L. Tri Devakul, a prominent Thai architect and developer, first discovered this almost deserted stretch of white sand and clear blue water in the late 1970s and was so struck by its charms that he built a simple thatched-roof holiday house on a nearby hill. Over the years since, the house has undergone many changes and so, with the growth of tourism, has Kata, though in both cases with remark-ably little effect on the pristine atmosphere that constitutes so much of its allure.

Kata, for instance, separated by a rocky prominence into Kata Yai ("Big Kata") and Kata Noi ("Little Kata") has acquired a number of low-rise hotels and lodges, begin-ning with the Club Méditerranée which extends along a considerable part of the larg-

er beach. M.L. Tri, who designed some of the club's buildings, bought a nearby piece of land for himself and in 1986 opened a restaurant. He called it the Boathouse after an old painted fishing boat that stood near its entrance. Basically a large, airy pavilion, the Boathouse proved a success not only with visitors but also with more permanent Phuket residents. It offered a variety of classic Thai dishes, most of them based on the abundant seafood caught daily in the Andaman Sea, served both in the pavilion and outside on a shady terrace overlooking the sea.

Food has remained a central part of the Boathouse's appeal, with a wide range of old favorites as well as specialities developed by the talented Executive Chef, Tummanoon Punchun. A sophisticated wine cellar, opened in the mid-90s, became the only one in Thailand selected for four consecutive years by the prestigious Wine Spectator. As a result, even during the low season, the restaurant is one of the most lively scenes on Phuket for superlative dining, drinking – and as a social gathering place par excellence.

The Boathouse Culinary Workshop, offering weekend cooking classes under the direction of Chef Tummanoon, began in the summer of 1994, mainly as a way of attracting low-season guests. Very quickly, however, it established itself as one of the most popular Thai cooking schools in the country, praised by critics in publications such as the Times of London, the New York Times, and the Los Angeles Times.

Chef Tummanoon favors a step-by-step, hands-on method of instruction, which he offers every Saturday and Sunday at the Boathouse to appreciative classes consisting of both hotel guests and outsiders.

Like all good cooks, he begins with an explanation of the basic ingredients, which in Thailand consist of a wide variety of herbs, spices, and vegetables that provide its special flavors – not just spicy hot but also sweet, sour, and salty in varying degrees to suit the particular dish. Some are familiar to outsiders, like chillies, garlic, coriander, spring onions, aubergine and cucumber.

Others may be exotic like aromatic lemongrass, Thai basil, galangal and the leaves and fruit of the kaffir lime. He then moves on to demonstrate the various methods of chopping, dicing and pounding in a mortar that precede the actual assembly of most dishes. Students learn these traditional techniques by taking part in the process with guidance from the chef and assistants. A total of ten recipes are learned during the two-day course. While most are standard Thai dishes, they have usually been given a special added touch by Chef Tummanoon and so have become personal creations of the Boathouse. Each recipe demonstrated in class has been selected for ease of preparation and adaptability to western kitchens.

Thai basil (*horapa*)   Lemon basil (*manglak*)   Holy basil (*kaprow*)

Basil is often used as a seasoning and garnish in Thai cooking. There are three varieties of basil that are used in Thai cuisine. **Thai basil** (*horapa*) tastes rather like anise, looks like sweet basil and is used in red and green curries. **Lemon basil** (*manglak*) has a lemony flavor, tiny leaves and is usually sprinkled over salads or used in soups. **Holy basil** or **hot basil** (*kaprow*) has a clove-like taste and purple-reddish tinged leaves. It doesn't store well, so buy just before you intend to use it. European basil can be used as a substitute for all varieties if you can't find the Thai varieties. Basil has a strong flavor, so don't use more than the recipe states.

Dried red chilies

Bird's-eye chilies

Fresh red chilies

Chillies are indispensable in Thai cooking and many different varieties are used. The large, finger-length green, red or yellow chilli is moderately hot. **Dried red chillies** of this variety are ground to make chilli flakes or ground red pepper. Tiny red, green or yellowy-orange **bird's-eye chillies**

are used in soups, curries and sauces, and are extremely hot. They are also available dried.

Chinese celery is much smaller with thinner stems than the normal Western variety and has a very intense, parsley-like flavor. The leaves and sometimes the stems are added to soups, rice dishes and stir-fried vegetables.

Coconut cream and **coconut milk** are used in many Thai desserts and curries. To obtain fresh coconut cream (which is normally used for desserts), grate the flesh of 1 coconut into a bowl (about 3 cups of grated coconut flesh), add $^1/_2$ cup water and knead thoroughly a few times, then strain with a muslin cloth or cheese cloth. **Thick coconut milk** is obtained by the same method but by adding double the water to the grated flesh (about 1 cup instead of $^1/_2$ cup). **Thin coconut milk** (which is used for curries rather than desserts) is obtained by pressing the coconut a second time, adding 1 cup of water to the same grated coconut flesh and squeezing it again. Although freshly pressed milk has more flavor, coconut cream and milk are now widely sold canned or in packets that are quick and convenient.

Coriander leaves with roots and stems

Coriander, also known as cilantro or Chinese parsley, is the most common herb used in Thai cooking. The whole plant is used—the root, stem and leaves. The seeds are roasted and then ground in a spice mill and used in curry pastes. The leaves are used for their fresh flavor, and as a garnish. For storage, wash and dry the fresh leaves before placing them in a plastic bag in the refrigerator—they will keep for 5 to 6 days.

Fish sauce is indispensable in Thai cooking. Made from salted, fermented fish or prawns,

good quality fish sauce is golden-brown in color and has a salty tang. It is used in the same way as the Chinese use soy sauce.

Galangal is a rhizome similar to ginger in appearance and a member of the same family. Known as *kha* in Thailand, *laos* in Indonesia and *lengkuas* in Singapore and Malaysia, it adds a distinctive fragrance and flavor to many Thai dishes. Dried galangal lacks the fragrance of fresh galangal, and most food stores now sell it fresh. It can be sliced and kept sealed in the freezer for several months.

Garlic chives or *ku chai*, also known as Chinese chives, have a far more emphatic, garlicky flavor than Western chives and resemble flat spring onions.

Green peppercorns are fresh peppercorn berries that are available still on the vine or bottled or canned in a brine. The peppercorns should be drained and rinsed before use. Thai and European varieties are readily available.

Kaffir lime is a small lime that has a very knobby and intensely fragrant skin, but virtually no juice. The skin or rind is often grated and added to dishes as a seasoning. The fragrant leaves are added whole to soups and curries, or finely shredded and added to salads or deep-fried fish cakes, giving a wonderfully tangy taste to these dishes. They are available frozen or dried in Asian food stores; frozen leaves are much more flavorful than the dried ones. The dried rind can be reconstituted and substituted for fresh.

Lemongrass, also known as citronella, is a lemon-scented stem which grows in clumps and is very important in Thai cooking. Each plant resembles a miniature leek. Use only the thicker bottom one third of the lemongrass stem. Remove and discard the dry outer leaves and use only the tender inner part of the plant. Lemongrass is available fresh, frozen or dried; fresh lemongrass is preferable because of its stronger smell and flavor.

Palm sugar is made from the distilled juice of various palm fruits (especially the coconut and arenga palms). Palm sugar varies in color from gold to dark brown. It has a rich flavor similar to dark brown sugar, molasses or maple syrup, which make good substitutes.

Fresh egg noodles
(*ba mee*)

Kway teow
(rice sticks or *hofun*)

Rice vermicelli
(*beehoon*)

Glass noodles
(*tang hoon*)

Noodles are available in many forms, and are made from either rice, wheat or mung bean flour. **Kway teow**, also known as rice sticks or *hofun*, are wide, flat rice-flour noodles sold fresh in Asian markets and available in dried form elsewhere. If fresh *kway teow* cannot be obtained, use **dried rice stick noodles** instead (these are thinner than kway teow and must be soaked in warm water for 10 minutes and drained before use). **Dried rice vermicelli** are very fine rice threads that must also be soaked before using. **Kanom jeen** are spaghetti-like rice-flour noodles which are similar to the laksa noodles of Malaysia and Singapore. **Egg noodles** (*ba mee*) are made from wheat flour. **Glass noodles**, also known as cellophane noodles, *tang hoon* or bean threads, are thin transparent noodles made from mung bean flour. They are sold in dried form and must be soaked in warm water briefly to soften.

Pandanus leaves come from a member of the pandanus palm or screw-pine family. Pandanus leaves are used as a wrapping for seasoned morsels of chicken or pork, and wrappers or flavoring for desserts. Look for fresh leaves at wet markets. One-ounce packages of dried leaves labeled "Dried Bay-Tovy Leaves" are exported from Thailand to overseas markets, but fresh leaves are preferred.

Preserved mustard cabbage or *mei cai*, is made from cooked bamboo or leaf mustard cabbages that are mixed with salt, sugar and dried. It is used largely as a flavoring rather than vegetables. Normally sold in sealed plastic bags, it can be stored refrigerated in an airtight container for about 6 months. This preserved vegetable should be soaked, rinsed and

squeezed in a couple of changes of water to remove the salt and odor before use.

Shrimp paste or *belacan* is a dense mixture of fermented group shrimp. It is sold in dried blocks and ranges in color from pink to blackish-brown. Shrimp paste should be slightly roasted to enhance its flavor before adding to other ingredients. Traditionally, it is wrapped in banana leaves and roasted over embers for a few minutes. Now it is commonly roasted directly over low flame using tongs for 30 seconds or heated in a frying-pan, wrapped in aluminium foil, for 1 to 2 minutes. Alternatively it can also be microwaved very quickly in a bowl covered with plastic for 30 seconds or so. Do not overcook the shrimp paste or it will scorch, become bitter and hollow.

Tamarind is a sour fruit that comes in a hard pod shell. Tamarind juice is one of the major souring agents in Thai cooking. To make tamarind juice, mix 1 tablespoon of dried tamarind pulp with 2 tablespoons warm water to soften, then mash well and strain to remove any seeds and fibers.

Turmeric is a member of the ginger family. This rhizome has a very rich yellow interior (which can stain clothing and plastic utensils) and a pleasant pungency that is absent in dried turmeric powder. Substitute $1/2$ teaspoon turmeric powder for 2 cm ($1/2$ in) fresh turmeric.

Spicy Seafood Salad (Yam Talay)

150 g (5 oz) fresh squids (4 to 5 small squids)
8 fresh medium prawns (about 150 g/5 oz), peeled and deveined
8 mussels in shells, scrubbed
8 fresh crab claws
200 g (7 oz) white fish fillets such as snapper or halibut, sliced
1 medium onion, thinly sliced
1 tomato, sliced
3 spring onions, cut into lengths
3 stalks (1 cup) Chinese celery, cut into lengths
4 large lettuce leaves, to serve

Dressing
2 tablespoons freshly squeezed lime juice
2 tablespoons fish sauce
1 tablespoon sugar
2 bird's-eye chillies, sliced
3 cloves garlic, minced
1 teaspoon Thai chilli sauce (Sriracha sauce)

Serves 4
Preparation time: **30 mins**
Cooking time: **5 mins**

1 To make the Dressing, combine all the ingredients in a small bowl and mix well, until the sugar is dissolved.

2 Rinse each squid thoroughly, detaching and discarding the head. Remove the cartilage in the center of the tentacles. Remove the reddish-brown skin from the body sac and scrape the inside of the body sac with the dull edge of a knife. Rinse well. Slice the body sac into rings. Pre-cook the squid pieces by steaming or stir-frying in a little oil for about 1 minute. Set aside.

3 Blanch the prawns in boiling water for 1 minute until just pink. Remove and set aside. Blanch the crab claws in the same manner. When cool, crack the claws and remove the shells.

4 In the same boiling water, cook the mussels until open. Drain and set aside to cool. Remove mussels from the shells.

5 Steam the fish fillets until they are opaque, but still moist. Set aside.

6 Toss the vegetables with the Dressing on a platter, then add all the seafood and gently toss to coat thoroughly with the Dressing. Line four plates with a large lettuce leaf each and arrange the salad on top. Spoon extra Dressing over and serve.

This dish can be made with squid only (Yam Pla-muk). In this case, substitute the seafood mixture with 500 g (1 lb) whole squid and prepare the recipe as above. Garnish with whole mint leaves.

Fragrant Glass Noodle Salad

60 g (2 oz) dried glass noodles (*tang hoon*)
12 fresh medium prawns (about 200 g/7 oz), peeled and
  deveined
150 g (5 oz) seafood (any combination of squid, fish, crab
  meat or clams), cut into bite-sized pieces
2 tablespoons freshly squeezed lime juice
2 tablespoons fish sauce
2 tablespoons shaved palm sugar or dark brown sugar
2 bird's-eye chillies, sliced
3 cloves garlic, minced
3 spring onions, cut into lengths
3 stalks (1 cup) Chinese celery, cut into lengths
8 large lettuce leaves, to serve
2 tablespoons ground roasted peanuts, to serve

1 Using a knife or kitchen shears, cut the dried glass
noodles into thirds. Blanch in boiling water for about 30
seconds until tender. Drain in a colander and set aside.
2 Poach the prawns and seafood in boiling water for
about 1 minute until just cooked through, being careful
not to overcook.
3 In a large bowl, combine the lime juice, fish sauce,
palm sugar, chillies and garlic and mix well. Add the
glass noodles, all the seafood, spring onions and celery
and toss thoroughly until all the dressing is absorbed.
4 Line a serving platter with the lettuce leaves and
arrange the salad on top. Garnish with ground peanuts
and serve.

Serves 4
Preparation time: **30 mins**
Cooking time: **10 mins**

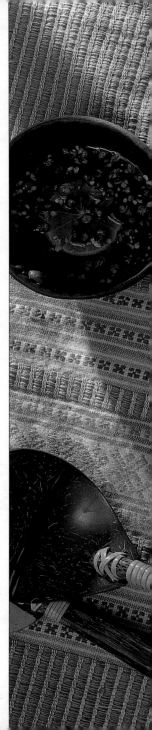

Minced Chicken and Prawns in an Egg Nest

2 eggs
2 tablespoons minced
  coriander leaves
1 to 2 bird's-eye chillies,
  thinly sliced
2 tablespoons oil

Filling
2 tablespoons oil
2 cloves garlic, minced
1 teaspoon crushed coriander roots and stems
1 teaspoon freshly ground
  black pepper
250 g (9 oz) fresh prawns,
  peeled, deveined and
  minced
250 g (9 oz) ground chicken
1 teaspoon salt
2 tablespoons shaved palm
  sugar or dark brown sugar
2 shallots, minced
4 tablespoons ground
  roasted peanuts

Serves 4
Preparation time: 30 mins
Cooking time: 30 mins

1 To make the Filling, heat the oil in a wok over medium heat and stir-fry the garlic, coriander roots and black pepper for 1 to 2 minutes until fragrant. Add the prawns and chicken and stir-fry until barely cooked, 2 to 3 minutes. Add the salt, palm sugar, shallots and peanuts. Stir-fry for another minute. Remove and set aside.

2 Beat the eggs in a bowl. Make a cone from a piece of banana leaf or waxed paper (or use a frosting cone). Pour a small amount of the beaten eggs into the cone. Lightly grease a crêpe or omelette pan with a bit of oil and heat over medium heat. Once the pan is hot, squeeze lines of the beaten eggs slowly onto the pan in a zig-zag pattern, shaping it into a 10-cm (4-in) square net. Once the egg has set, carefully remove from the pan with a spatula and set aside to cool.

3 When cool enough to handle, place a small amount of coriander leaves and chillies in the center of each egg net. Then place 2 teaspoons of the Filling on top and fold the sides toward the center. Fold in the remaining sides to make a small square package. Serve immediately.

4 A simple alternative to the egg nest is to prepare a very thin omelette. Cut the omelette into the required number of squares, place the coriander leaves, chillies and Filling onto each square and fold to make a small package.

Stir-fry the Filling ingredients in a wok.

Make a cone from a piece of banana leaf or waxed paper (or use a frosting cone).

Squeeze lines of the beaten eggs in a zig-zag pattern to form a 10-cm (4-in) square net.

Fold the egg nest over the Filling to make a small package.

Tom Yam Soup (Spicy Prawn Tamarind Soup)

1 1/2 liters (6 cups) chicken stock or 3 chicken stock cubes in 1 1/2 liters (6 cups) boiling water
2 stalks lemongrass, thick bottom part only, outer leaves removed, sliced
4 to 6 bird's-eye chillies, sliced
3 cm (1 in) galangal root, thinly sliced
8 kaffir lime leaves, sliced
4 tablespoons fish sauce
12 to 16 fresh medium prawns (250 g/9 oz)
250 g (2 cups) fresh or canned straw or button mushrooms
4 tablespoons freshly squeezed lime juice
1 tablespoon Roasted Chilli Paste (see below)

Roasted Chilli Paste
12 dried red chillies
5 whole shallots, unpeeled
8 cloves garlic, unpeeled
2 tablespoons dried shrimp paste
2 tablespoons dried prawns, soaked in warm water for 10 minutes to soften
2 tablespoons shaved palm sugar or dark brown sugar
2 tablespoons fish sauce
2 tablespoons tamarind juice (page 7)
1 tablespoon oil

1 To make the Roasted Chilli Paste, dry-fry the dried chillies in a wok or frying-pan over low heat until dark and fragrant, taking care not to burn. When cool, remove the stems from the chillies, discard the seeds and cut the chillies into lengths. Set aside.

2 In the same pan, dry-fry the shallots and garlic over low heat until soft and blistered. This should take about 3 to 5 minutes. Set aside to cool. Peel and slice the garlic and shallots.

3 Roast the shrimp paste over low flame using tongs or aluminium foil (see page 7).

4 Place the dried prawns into a mortar or blender and grind to a coarse powder. Add the chillies, garlic and shallots and grind until fine. Add the shrimp paste, palm sugar, fish sauce and tamarind juice and grind to a smooth paste.

5 Heat the oil in a wok or skillet over medium heat. Add the chilli paste and stir-fry until deep brown and very fragrant. This makes about 125 ml (1/2 cup) of paste. When cool, the paste can be stored in a tightly sealed container in the fridge for 3 to 5 days.

6 To make the soup, bring the chicken stock to a boil in a stockpot over high heat. Add the lemongrass, chillies, galangal and lime leaves and simmer for 1 to 2 minutes. Then add the fish sauce, prawns and mushrooms. Reduce heat to medium and gradually stir in the lime juice and Roasted Chilli Paste. Simmer for 2 to 3 minutes until the prawns turn pink, but do not overcook. Check seasoning, adding more fish sauce or lime juice for a hot and piquant soup. Serve immediately.

Serves 4
Preparation time: **15 mins**
Cooking time: 30 mins

Spicy Coconut Chicken or Seafood Soup

1 liter (4 cups) thin coconut milk
750 ml (3 cups) chicken stock or 1 1/2 chicken stock cubes in 750 ml (3 cups) boiling water
6 kaffir lime leaves, sliced
1 cm (1/2 in) galangal root, thinly sliced
3 bird's-eye chillies
1 stalk lemongrass, thick bottom part only, tough outer layers discarded
300 g (10 oz) fresh boneless chicken or seafood, sliced into thin strips

16 fresh or canned straw or button mushrooms
4 tablespoons freshly squeezed lime juice
2 tablespoons fish sauce
2 spring onions, cut into lengths, to serve
Few sprigs coriander leaves

Serves 4
Preparation time: **10 mins**
Cooking time: **10 mins**

1 Heat coconut milk and chicken stock in a stockpot over medium heat for 3 minutes. Do not allow to boil.
2 Add the lime leaves, galangal, chillies and lemongrass.
3 Stir in the chicken or seafood and mushrooms. Cook until the soup just begins to boil. Turn off heat. Add the lime juice and fish sauce. Mix well. Remove and serve hot, garnished with spring onions and coriander leaves.

Clear Vegetable Soup with Prawns

$^1/_2$ teaspoon dried shrimp paste, roasted (page 7)
1 cm ($^1/_2$ in) galangal root
1 shallot
$^1/_2$ teaspoon black peppercorns
1$^1/_2$ liters (6 cups) chicken stock or 3 chicken stock cubes in 1$^1/_2$ liters (6 cups) boiling water
2 tablespoons grated pumpkin or carrot
60 g ($^1/_2$ cup) baby corn
20 fresh or canned straw or button mushrooms
2 iceberg lettuce leaves

12 fresh medium prawns (about 200 g/7 oz), peeled and deveined
2 tablespoons fish sauce
1 teaspoon sugar
2 sprigs Thai basil leaves, to serve

Serves 4
Preparation time: **15 mins**
Cooking time: **10 mins**

1 Grind the shrimp paste, galangal root, shallot and black peppercorns in a blender to a smooth paste.
2 Bring the chicken stock to a boil in a stockpot. Stir in the spice paste and mix well. Add the pumpkin, baby corn, mushrooms and lettuce. Simmer over medium heat until the vegetables are cooked. Then add the prawns, fish sauce and sugar. Mix well. When the prawns turn pink, remove from heat and stir in the basil leaves.

Clear Soup with Chicken or Seafood

1½ liters (6 cups) chicken stock or 3 chicken stock cubes in 1½ liters (6 cups) boiling water
4 cloves garlic, sliced
250 g (9 oz) fresh chicken breast or seafood, cut into thin strips
60 g (1 cup) coarsely chopped lettuce
3 tablespoons soy sauce
4 tablespoons fish sauce
Pinch of freshly ground black pepper
2 sprigs coriander leaves, to serve
2 spring onions, green tops cut into lengths, to serve
1 teaspoon Crispy Fried Garlic (see Note), to serve

1 Bring the chicken stock and garlic to a boil in a stockpot over high heat. Then reduce heat to medium and let the mixture simmer for about 3 minutes.
2 Add the chicken or seafood, lettuce, soy sauce, fish sauce and black pepper and simmer for 5 more minutes, stirring constantly, until the chicken is cooked.
3 Serve hot, garnished with the coriander leaves, spring onions and Crispy Fried Garlic.

Crispy Fried Garlic is readily available in packets or jars in most wet markets, supermarkets and provision shops. To make it at home, thinly slice several cloves of garlic as desired and stir-fry in a few tablespoons of hot oil over low heat for 1 to 2 minutes, stirring constantly, until golden brown and crispy. Remove with a slotted spoon and drain the excess oil on paper towels.

Serves 4
Preparation time: **20 mins**
Cooking time: **10 mins**

Turmeric Soup with Chicken or Fish

4 shallots
2 cm (1 in) fresh turmeric root, sliced
1 stalk lemongrass, thick bottom part only, outer layers discarded, sliced
2 cm (1 in) galangal root
2 teaspoons crushed coriander roots and stems
$1^1/_2$ liters (6 cups) chicken stock or 3 chicken stock cubes in $1^1/_2$ liters (6 cups) boiling water
350 g (12 oz) boneless fish fillets or chicken, sliced
4 teaspoons sugar
3 tablespoons fish sauce
1 spring onion, green part cut into lengths, to serve

1 Grind the shallots, turmeric root, lemongrass, galangal root and coriander roots to a smooth paste in a blender.
2 Heat the chicken stock in a stockpot over high heat. Stir in the spice paste and bring to a boil. Reduce heat to medium and add the fish or chicken. Let the mixture simmer for about 3 minutes, stirring occasionally, until cooked. Then add the sugar and fish sauce. Mix well and remove from heat.
3 Serve immediately, garnished with the spring onions.

Serves 4
Preparation time: 20 mins
Cooking time: 10 mins

Spicy Lemongrass Soup with Grilled Prawns

3 dried red chillies
2 shallots
2 cloves garlic
8 to 12 fresh large prawns
  (about 300 g/10 oz)
1¹/₂ liters (6 cups) chicken
  stock or 3 chicken stock
  cubes in 1¹/₂ liters (6
  cups) boiling water
3 stalks lemongrass, thick
  bottom part only, tough
  outer layers discarded,
  thinly sliced
4 thin slices galangal root
3 kaffir lime leaves, sliced
2 teaspoons crushed
  coriander roots and stems
4 tablespoons fish sauce
2 tablespoons tamarind
  juice (page 7)
2 teaspoons sugar
2 sprigs coriander leaves,
  to serve

1 In a wok or frying-pan, dry-fry the dried chillies over low heat until dark and fragrant. When cool, remove stems and deseed. Set aside

2 In the same wok or pan, dry-fry the shallots and garlic over low heat for 3 to 5 minutes until soft and blistered. When cool, slice the shallots and garlic. Set aside.

3 Grill the prawns on a charcoal or pan grill over medium heat until pink on both sides. This should take about 3 to 5 minutes. Transfer to a plate and set aside.

4 Heat the chicken stock in a stockpot over high heat and bring to a boil. Reduce heat to medium and add the lemongrass, galangal root, lime leaves, roasted dried chillies, coriander roots, roasted shallots and garlic. Simmer uncovered for about 5 minutes, stirring constantly, then add the grilled prawns and stir in the fish sauce, tamarind juice and sugar. Mix well and remove from heat.

5 Serve hot, garnished with coriander leaves.

Serves 4
Preparation time: **40 mins**
Cooking time: **15 mins**

Grill the prawns until pink on both sides.

Slice the lemongrass, galangal root, kaffir lime leaves, coriander roots, shallots and garlic.

Add ingredients to the Chicken Stock and simmer for about 5 minutes, stirring constantly.

Add the grilled prawns, fish sauce, tamarind juice and sugar, and mix well before serving.

Pad Thai
(Stir-fried Rice Stick Noodles)

4 tablespoons oil
4 shallots, minced
12 to 16 fresh medium prawns (about 250 g or 9 oz),
  peeled and deveined
4 eggs
250 g (9 oz) dried rice stick noodles (*kway teow* or *hofun*),
  soaked in warm water until soft and drained
1 teaspoon dried chilli flakes
200 g (3 cups) bean sprouts
1 small bunch garlic chives (*ku chai*), cut into lengths
4 tablespoons ground roasted peanuts
2 limes, halved, to serve

Sauce
2 tablespoons tamarind juice (page 7)
2 tablespoons shaved palm sugar or dark brown sugar
2 tablespoons fish sauce
$1/_2$ teaspoon white pepper
Pinch of salt

1 Combine all the Sauce ingredients in a wok or saucepan.
Cook for 1 to 2 minutes over medium heat, stirring constantly, until the sugar is dissolved. Set aside.
2 Heat the oil in a wok over medium heat. Add the shallots and stir-fry for about 1 minute until fragrant. Add
the prawns and stir-fry until pink. Reduce heat and add
the eggs. Mix well and add the rice noodles. Increase heat
and stir-fry for about 1 minute. Add the Sauce ingredients
and chilli flakes. Mix well and stir-fry for 30 seconds to 1
minute. Finally, add half the bean sprouts and chives and
stir-fry for another 30 seconds before removing from heat.
3 Serve hot on individual plates, garnished with the remaining fresh bean sprouts and chives, peanuts and limes.

*This dish may also be prepared with meat or mixed seafood
instead of prawns. Simply substitute 300 g (10 oz) mixed
seafood, chicken, pork or beef.*

Serves 4
Preparation time: **10 mins**
Cooking time: **10 mins**

Classic Thai Fried Rice

500 g (4 cups) cooked rice
4 tablespoons oil
5 cloves garlic, minced
250 g (9 oz) chicken, pork
  or beef, thinly sliced
2 eggs
4 tablespoons soy sauce
1 teaspoon sugar
$1/2$ teaspoon white pepper
2 spring onions, thinly
  sliced
1 cucumber, peeled and
  sliced, to serve
2 tomatoes, cut into
  wedges, to serve
1 lime, halved, to serve

Chilli Dipping Sauce

4 tablespoons freshly
  squeezed lime juice
3 tablespoons fish sauce
2 bird's-eye chillies, thinly
  sliced
2 cloves garlic, minced

Serves 4
Preparation time: **20 mins**
Cooking time: **12 mins**

1 Make the Chilli Dipping Sauce first by combining all the ingredients in a bowl, stirring to mix well. This makes about 175 ml ($3/4$ cup) of sauce. Transfer to a serving bowl and set aside.

2 Place the rice in a large bowl and toss it gently to separate the grains. Set aside.

3 Heat the oil in a wok over high heat, turning to grease the sides. Add the garlic and stir-fry for about 1 minute until fragrant. Add the meat and stir-fry for 1 to 2 minutes until the meat changes color, then add the eggs and mix well. Add the rice and stir-fry for several minutes, mixing and tossing constantly until the rice is heated through. Finally add the soy sauce, sugar and pepper. Stir-fry for a further 1 to 2 minutes and remove from heat.

4 Arrange the rice on a serving platter and scatter spring onions on top. Serve immediately with cucumber, tomatoes, lime and Chilli Dipping Sauce.

This dish always works better with cooked rice prepared a day or two in advance. So consider making extra rice whenever you cook for another meal.

Pineapple Fried Rice

250 g (9 oz) fresh squids (6 to 7 small squids)
500 g (4 cups) cooked rice
1 large fresh pineapple
4 tablespoons oil
2 cloves garlic, minced
2 medium onions, chopped
1 tablespoon curry powder
8 fresh medium prawns (about 150 g/5 oz), peeled and
  deveined
150 g (5 oz) fresh or canned crab meat (about 1 cup)
1 green or red bell pepper, diced
1 tomato, diced
4 tablespoons yellow raisins
1 teaspoon sugar
2 tablespoons soy sauce
$3/_4$ teaspoon white pepper

1 Clean the squids (see page 8) and slice into thin strips.
2 Place the rice in a large bowl and toss it gently to separate the grains. Set aside.
3 With the sharp point of a knife, mark a rectangular outline on the pineapple and cut into the pineapple along these lines. Remove the rectangular section and hollow out the fruit in the center, creating a bowl but not cutting through. Dice 125 g of the pineapple (about $3/_4$ cup). Set aside.
4 Heat the oil in a wok over medium heat, turning to grease the sides. Add the garlic and stir-fry until fragrant, about 1 minute, then add the onions and curry powder. When fragrant, add the seafood and stir-fry until the prawns turn pink and are just cooked.
5 Add the rice, diced pineapple, bell pepper, tomato and raisins. Mix well and stir-fry for about 3 minutes. Season with the sugar, soy sauce and pepper. Stir-fry for another minute until well mixed before removing from heat.
6 Serve the fried rice in the pineapple as shown.

Serves 4
Preparation time: **30 mins**
Cooking time: **15 mins**

Stir-fried Kway Teow with Crab

2 fresh medium crabs
(about 1 1/2 kg/3 lbs)
4 tablespoons oil
4 shallots, sliced
4 eggs
250 g (9 oz) dried rice stick
noodles (*kway teow* or
hofun), soaked in warm
water until soft and
drained
2 spring onions, thinly
sliced, to serve
1 red chilli, thinly sliced,
to serve

Sauce
2 tablespoons soy sauce
2 tablespoons oyster sauce
2 teaspoons sugar
1/2 teaspoon white pepper

1 Detach the claws from each crab. Lift off the carapace and discard. Scrape out any roe and discard the gills. Rinse well and quarter the crab. Trim the legs.
2 Combine all the Sauce ingredients in a bowl. Mix well until the sugar is dissolved. Set aside.
3 Heat the oil in a wok over high heat. Add the shallots and stir-fry for about 1 minute until fragrant. Add the eggs and scramble until just cooked. Add the crabs and continue to stir-fry for a further minute.
4 Add the rice noodles and stir-fry until soft. Season with the Sauce ingredients, mix well and remove from heat.
5 Serve immediately on individual plates, garnished with spring onions and chili.

Serves 4
Preparation time: 20 to 30 mins
Cooking time: 8 mins

Stir-fried Kway Teow with Vegetables

4 tablespoons oil
3 cloves garlic, minced
150 g (5 oz) ground beef, pork or chicken
1 egg
100 g (1 cup) baby corn
100 g (1 cup) cauliflower florets
100 g (1 cup) asparagus, cut into lengths
100 g (1 cup) Chinese broccoli (*kailan*), cut into lengths
250 g (9 oz) dried rice stick noodles (*kway teow* or *hofun*), soaked in warm water until soft and drained

Sauce
1 tablespoon fish sauce
1 tablespoon oyster sauce
1 teaspoon sugar
1 teaspoon black soy sauce
$^1/_2$ teaspoon white pepper

1 Combine all the Sauce ingredients in a bowl. Stir until well mixed and the sugar is dissolved. Set aside.
2 Heat the oil in a wok over high heat. Add the garlic and stir-fry for about 1 minute until fragrant. Add the ground meat. Continue to stir-fry until the meat changes color, then add the egg and mix well.
3 Add the vegetables and stir-fry for 2 to 3 minutes until tender and cooked. Add the rice noodles, season with the Sauce ingredients and stir-fry until well mixed, 2 to 3 minutes. Remove from heat and serve hot.

Serves 4
Preparation time: **10 mins**
Cooking time: **5 to 10 mins**

Chicken with Thai Basil and Vegetables (Gai Khee Maw)

2 tablespoons oil
3 cloves garlic, minced
2 bird's-eye chillies, sliced
2 tablespoons fresh green peppercorns (optional)
300 g (10 oz) fresh chicken breast, cut into thin strips
120 g (4 oz) baby corn (about 1 1/2 cups)
8 dried black Chinese mushrooms, soaked in warm water
  for 20 minutes, stems discarded and caps sliced
100 g (1 cup) green beans, tops and tails removed,
  cut into lengths
125 g (1 1/2 cups) cauliflower florets
3 red chillies, thinly sliced diagonally
1 tablespoon fish sauce
1 tablespoon oyster sauce
1 tablespoon sugar
1/2 teaspoon freshly ground black pepper
125 ml (1/2 cup) chicken stock or 1/4 chicken stock cube
  in 125 ml (1/2 cup) boiling water
2 sprigs (1/2 cup) Thai basil leaves

1 Heat the oil in a wok or frying-pan over high heat. Add the garlic, bird's-eye chillies and green peppercorns. Stir-fry until the garlic turns golden brown and fragrant.
2 Add the chicken, baby corn, mushrooms, green beans, cauliflower and chillies, and stir-fry for about 5 minutes until the chicken is cooked and the vegetables are tender. Then season with the fish sauce, oyster sauce, sugar and black pepper. Mix well and add the chicken stock. Stir-fry for a further minute, add the basil leaves and remove from heat.
3 Serve hot with steamed rice.

Serves 4
Preparation time: 10 mins
Cooking time: 10 mins

Marinated Chicken Chunks

3 boneless chicken thighs
(400 g), cut into pieces
12 pandanus leaf cups or
12 pieces tracing paper
(each 15 x 20 cm/6 x 8 in)
Oil for deep frying

Marinade
1 teaspoon sesame seeds
1 teaspoon sesame oil
1 teaspoon fish sauce
1 teaspoon soy sauce
1 teaspoon crushed coriander roots and stems

1 teaspoon minced garlic
1 teaspoon grated ginger
2 teaspoons shaved palm
sugar or brown sugar
Pinch of white pepper

Sesame Sauce
1 tablespoon sesame oil
2 tablespoons tamarind
juice (page 7)
$2^1/_2$ tablespoons sugar
1 tablespoon oyster sauce
1 tablespoon fish sauce
1 teaspoon sesame seeds

1 Pour all the ingredients for Marinade over the chicken pieces. Mix well and marinate for at least 1 hour.
2 To make the Sesame Sauce, bring the sesame oil, tamarind juice, sugar, oyster sauce and fish sauce to a boil in a saucepan over medium heat. Add the sesame seeds and remove from heat. Set aside.
3 Place the marinated chicken pieces into the leaf cups (as shown in the photo) or wrap in the tracing paper to form small parcels. Deep-fry in medium hot oil for about 7 minutes each until golden brown. Remove and serve with the Sesame Sauce.

Serves 4
Preparation time: 1 hour   Cooking time: **20 mins**

Marinate the chicken pieces for at least 1 hour (overnight is better).

Form small cups with the pandanus leaves, using toothpicks or staples to fasten the sides.

Place the marinated chicken meat pieces into the pandanus leaf parcels.

Lower gently in a wire basket and deep-fry in medium hot oil until golden brown.

Green Curry Chicken

250 ml (1 cup) thick coconut milk
3 tablespoons Green Curry Paste (page 56)
500 g (1 lb) fresh chicken breast, cut into bite-sized pieces
750 ml (3 cups) thin coconut milk
8 kaffir lime leaves, sliced
125 g (1$^1/_2$ cups) eggplant, cut into cubes
4 red chillies, sliced
3 tablespoons fish sauce
1$^1/_2$ tablespoons shaved palm sugar or dark brown sugar
20 Thai basil leaves

1 Heat the thick coconut milk in a pot for about 2 minutes over medium heat. Stir continuously and do not allow to boil. Add the Green Curry Paste and continue stirring until the mixture is thick and fragrant. Add the chicken and one third of the thin coconut milk. Bring to a boil and gradually stir in the remaining thin coconut milk.
2 Add the kaffir lime leaves, eggplant and chillies (leave some chillies for garnishing). Simmer for about 10 minutes until the curry is thickened. Add the fish sauce, palm sugar and basil leaves. Stir to blend thoroughly before removing from heat.
3 Garnish with the reserved chillies and serve with steamed rice.

Serves 4
Preparation time: **30 mins**
Cooking time: **20 mins**

Heat the thick coconut milk in a pot and stir in the Green Curry Paste.

Add the chicken and one third of the thin coconut milk. Bring to a boil.

Add all the remaining ingredients and stir well.

*Add the fish sauce, palm sugar and basil.
Blend thoroughly and remove from heat.*

Roast Duck in Red Curry

500 ml (2 cups) chicken stock or 1 chicken stock cube in 500 ml (2 cups) boiling water
500 ml (2 cups) thin coconut milk
4 tablespoons Red Curry Paste (page 46)
3 tablespoons fish sauce
3 teaspoons sugar
125 g (1 1/2 cups) eggplant, sliced
125 g (1 cup) seedless grapes or pineapple chunks
15 cherry tomatoes
1 red chilli, sliced
6 kaffir lime leaves, thinly sliced
10 basil leaves, sliced
300 g (10 oz) Chinese roast duck

1 To make the curry sauce, heat the chicken stock and half of the coconut milk in a wok or pot over medium heat for 2 to 3 minutes. Do not allow to boil. Stir in the Red Curry Paste. Then add the remaining coconut milk and season with the fish sauce and sugar. Mix well and cook for a minute to allow the sugar to dissolve. Add the eggplant and cook until tender. Add the grapes or pineapple chunks, tomatoes, chilli, kaffir lime leaves and basil leaves. Simmer for about 3 minutes until the sauce is thickened.

2 Slice the roast duck and add to the curry. Simmer for a further minute. Remove from heat and serve with steamed rice.

Serves 4
Preparation time: **15 mins**
Cooking time: **15 mins**

This delicious curry combines Chinese roast duck with spices and fragrant herbs.

Serve family style in a casserole or pot, or in individual portions (shown at right).

Grilled Lobster with Spicy Basil Garlic Sauce

700 g (1 $^1/_2$ lbs) fresh lobsters, crayfish or king
prawns, shelled and
cleaned
Pinch of salt and pepper
2 tablespoons Crispy Fried
Basil Leaves (see Note),
to serve

Spicy Basil Garlic Sauce
2 tablespoons oil
4 cloves garlic, sliced
1 to 2 bird's-eye chillies
2 red chillies, sliced
1 tablespoon oyster sauce
1 tablespoon fish sauce
1 teaspoon sugar
10 basil leaves, sliced
$^1/_2$ teaspoon cornflour in
1 tablespoon water

Serves 4
Preparation time: 20 mins
Cooking time: 10 mins

1 To make the Spicy Basil Garlic Sauce, heat the oil in a wok or saucepan over medium heat. Add the garlic and both types of chillies and stir-fry for 1 to 2 minutes until fragrant. Add the oyster sauce, fish sauce and basil, and stir-fry for a further minute until well mixed. Add the cornflour mixture and cook for another 30 seconds until the sauce is thickened. Remove from heat and set aside.
2 Rub the salt and pepper onto the lobsters or prawns. Grill on a charcoal or pan grill or under the broiler for several minutes on each side until cooked. Place on a serving platter.
3 Spread the Spicy Basil Garlic Sauce over the grilled seafood. Serve hot, garnished with Crispy Fried Basil Leaves.

*To make the **Crispy Fried Basil Leaves**, stir-fry 8 to 10 thin-ly sliced or whole basil leaves in several tablespoons of hot oil over medium heat for 1 to 2 minutes, stirring constantly, until crispy and fragrant. Remove with a slotted spoon and drain the excess oil on paper towels.*

To make the Spicy Basil Garlic Sauce, heat oil and add sliced garlic and chillies.

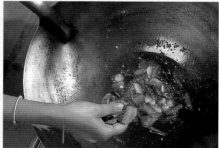

Season with the oyster sauce, fish sauce, sugar and basil leaves.

Rub the lobsters with salt and pepper and grill over medium heat on both sides until cooked.

Pour the sauce over the grilled lobsters and garnish with Crispy Fried Basil Leaves.

Pan-fried Fish with Tom Yam Sauce

Oil for deep-frying
1 tablespoon minced
  galangal root
1 tablespoon very thinly
  sliced kaffir lime leaves
1 tablespoon thinly sliced
  lemongrass
600 g (1$^1/_4$ lbs) white fish
  fillets
5 tablespoons flour, mixed
  with $^1/_2$ teaspoon salt
  and $^1/_2$ teaspoon white
  pepper

Tom Yam Sauce
1 stalk lemongrass, thick
  bottom part only, outer
  layers discarded, sliced
1 cm ($^1/_2$ in) galangal
  root, sliced
3 kaffir lime leaves, sliced
1 bird's-eye chilli, sliced
2 dried chillies, soaked in
  warm water for 10 min-
  utes to soften, stems discarded and deseeded
2 tablespoons oil
250 ml (1 cup) chicken
  stock or $^1/_2$ chicken stock
  cube in 250 ml (1 cup)
  boiling water
2 teaspoons sugar
2 tablespoons fish sauce
60 ml ($^1/_4$ cup) cream
2 teaspoons freshly
  squeezed lime juice

1 To make the Tom Yam Sauce, grind the lemongrass, galangal, lime leaves, fresh chilli and dried chillies to a smooth paste in a blender. Heat the oil in a saucepan over medium heat, stir-fry the paste for 1 to 2 minutes until fragrant. Add the chicken stock, sugar, fish sauce and cream, and simmer until the sugar is dissolved. Finally, season with the lime juice. If the sauce is too thick, dilute with some water.

2 Heat 3 tablespoons oil in a wok or pan over high heat. Add the minced galangal and stir-fry until crispy and fragrant, 1 to 2 minutes. Remove with a slotted spoon and set aside. In the same wok or pan, stir-fry the lime leaves and lemongrass separately in the same manner. Remove and set aside.

3 Lightly coat the fish fillets with the seasoned flour. Deep-fry in a wok or pan over high heat for 3 to 5 minutes until crispy. Remove and drain the excess oil on paper towels.

4 Sprinkle the crispy fried galangal, lime leaves and lemongrass on top of the fish. Pour the Tom Yam Sauce over and serve hot.

Serves 4
Preparation time: **45 mins**
Cooking time: **15 mins**

Grilled Prawns with Sweet and Sour Chilli Sauce

700 g (1 1/2 lbs) fresh tiger prawns (about 8 to 10), head trimmed, sliced open and deveined
Pinch of salt and white pepper
Few sprigs coriander leaves, to garnish

Sweet and Sour Chilli Sauce
1 tablespoon oil
5 cloves garlic, minced
2 to 3 bird's-eye chillies, thinly sliced
1 teaspoon crushed coriander roots and stems
80 ml (1/3 cup) white vinegar
1 tablespoon sugar
2 tablespoons shaved palm sugar or dark brown sugar
2 tablespoons fish sauce
2 tablespoons tamarind juice (page 7)
125 ml (1/2 cup) chicken stock or 1/4 chicken stock cube in 125 ml (1/2 cup) boiling water

1 To make the Sweet and Sour Chilli Sauce, heat the oil in a wok or saucepan over medium heat and add the garlic, chillies and coriander roots. Stir-fry for about a minute until fragrant. Add the vinegar, sugar, fish sauce, tamarind juice and chicken stock. Mix well and simmer for about 5 minutes. Remove from heat and set aside. This makes about 375 ml (1 cup) of sauce.
2 Rub the salt and pepper onto the prawns. Grill on a charcoal or pan grill over medium heat until pink on both sides, 5 to 10 minutes. Transfer to a serving platter.
3 Pour the Sweet and Sour Chilli Sauce over the grilled prawns. Garnish with coriander leaves and serve hot.

Serves 4
Preparation time: **15 mins**
Cooking time: **20 mins**

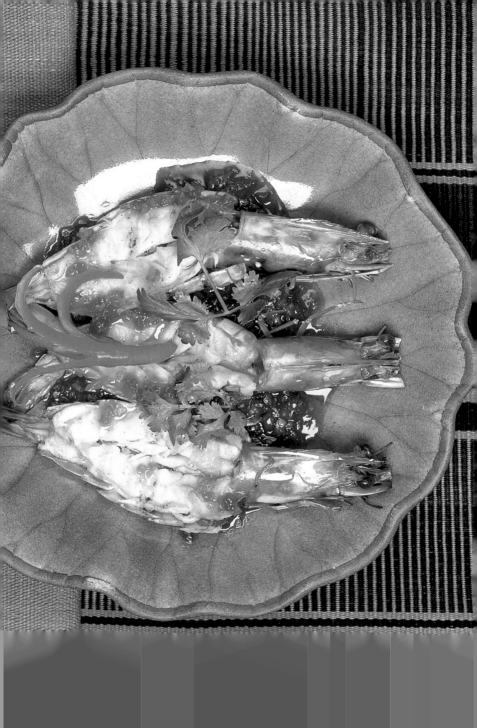

Crispy Crab Claws (Poo Krob)

10 to 12 fresh crab claws, cracked and cleaned
150 g (5 oz) fresh or canned crab meat (about 1 cup)
6 cloves garlic, minced
2 teaspoons crushed coriander roots and stems
2 teaspoons oyster sauce
2 tablespoons fish sauce
$1/_2$ teaspoon white pepper
2 egg yolks
40 g ($2/_3$ cup) breadcrumbs
Oil for deep-frying
Thai or Chinese plum sauce, for dipping
1 to 2 limes, cut into wedges, to serve

1 Crack the claws and carefully remove the meat reserving the claws and shells.
2 Mix the crab meat, garlic, coriander roots, oyster sauce, fish sauce and pepper thoroughly. Add enough egg yolks to bind the mixture.
3 Grease your hands with oil and shape the crab meat mixture around the claws.
4 Roll the claws in the breadcrumbs to coat.
5 Heat the oil in a wok to medium hot. Gently lower the claws into the oil and cook until golden brown, about 7 minutes each. Remove and drain on paper towels.
6 Serve with plum sauce and limes.

Serves 4
Preparation time: **20 mins**
Cooking time: **10 to 15 mins**

Add egg yolks to bind the crab meat mixture.

Shape the mixture around each claw.

Roll the claws in the breadcrumbs.

Lower the claws gently into the oil and cook until golden brown.

Red Seafood Curry

500 ml (2 cups) thick
coconut milk
2 tablespoons Red Curry
Paste (see below)
2$^1/_2$ tablespoons fish sauce
1 tablespoon shaved palm
sugar or dark brown
sugar
500 g (1 lb) seafood (any
combination of fish,
prawns, crab meat or
clams), cut into bite-sized
pieces
4 kaffir lime leaves, thinly
sliced
2 red chillies, sliced

Red Curry Paste
1 tablespoon dried shrimp
paste
5 to 6 dried red chillies
(about $^1/_2$ cup)
3 to 4 shallots
2 cloves garlic
2 teaspoons grated kaffir
lime peel
4 stalks lemongrass, bot-
tom thick part only, outer
leaves discarded, sliced
1 coriander root and stem
5 cm (2 in) galangal root,
sliced

1 To make the Red Curry Paste, roast shrimp paste over low flame using tongs or aluminium foil (see page 7).
2 In a wok or frying-pan, dry-fry the dried chillies over low heat until dark and fragrant. When cool, remove stems, discard the seeds and cut the chillies into lengths.
3 In the same wok or frying-pan, dry-fry the shallots and garlic over low heat for 3 to 5 minutes until soft and blistered. When cool, slice and set aside.
4 Grind the lime peel, lemongrass, coriander root and galangal root to a paste in a blender or spice grinder. Add the roasted chillies, shallots, garlic and shrimp paste. Grind to a smooth paste. This makes about 250 ml (1 cup) of paste. The paste can be stored in an airtight container in the fridge for a month or in the freezer for up to 3 months.
5 To make the curry, heat the coconut milk in a wok or saucepan over medium heat. Do not overcook as the coconut oil may separate. Stir in the Red Curry Paste and cook for 2 minutes. Season with the fish sauce and palm sugar and simmer for about 3 minutes until the curry is thickened.
6 Add the seafood and half of the kaffir lime leaves. Simmer until the seafood is cooked, about 3 minutes. Adjust for seasoning, adding more fish sauce, sugar or Red Curry Paste if desired. Remove from heat and stir in the remaining kaffir lime leaves and chillies. Serve immediately.

Serves 4
Preparation time: **45 mins**
Cooking time: **30 mins**

Deep-fried Fish with Hot Basil and Chilli Sauce

1 whole fresh fish (about
450 g/1 lb), deboned
4 tablespoons flour, mixed
with a pinch of salt and
white pepper
Oil for deep-frying

Hot Basil and Chilli Sauce
1 tablespoon oil
3 cloves garlic, minced
2 red chillies, sliced
1 tablespoon sugar
1 tablespoon oyster sauce
1 tablespoon fish sauce
1 tablespoon soy sauce
1 teaspoon white pepper
10 basil leaves

1 To make the Hot Basil and Chilli Sauce, heat the oil in a
wok or saucepan over medium heat. Add the garlic and
chillies and stir-fry for about 1 minute until fragrant. Add
the sugar, oyster sauce, fish sauce, soy sauce and pepper,
and stir-fry for a further minute. Finally add the basil
leaves, mix well and quickly remove from heat. Set aside.
2 Dip the fish in the flour mixture to coat thoroughly.
Heat the oil in a wok over high heat. Deep-fry the fish for
3 to 5 minutes until golden brown and crispy. Remove
and drain the excess oil on paper towels. Place on a serving platter.
3 Pour the Hot Basil and Chilli Sauce over the deep-fried
fish and serve immediately.

Serves 4
Preparation time: **10 mins**
Cooking time: **10 mins**

Stir-fried Baby Clams in Roasted Chilli Paste

3 tablespoons oil
4 cloves garlic, minced
1¹/₂ tablespoons Roasted
  Chilli Paste (page 14)
1 kg (2 lbs) fresh clams
2 spring onions, cut into
  lengths
4 tablespoons minced
  onion
2 tablespoons soy sauce
2 tablespoons fish sauce
1 tablespoon sugar
¹/₂ teaspoon freshly
  ground black pepper
1 to 2 red chillies, thinly
  sliced
30 basil leaves

125 ml (¹/₂ cup) chicken
  stock or ¹/₄ chicken stock
  cube in 125 ml (¹/₂ cup)
  boiling water

1 Scrub the clams, then soak and drain in a couple of changes of water to remove the soil trapped in the clams.
2 Heat the oil in a wok over high heat. Add the garlic and Roasted Chilli Paste and stir-fry for 30 seconds until fragrant. Add the clams and stir-fry until just open.
3 Add the rest of the ingredients and continue to stir-fry for 2 minutes. Remove from heat and serve hot.

Serves 4
Preparation time: **10 mins**
Cooking time: **5 mins**

Southern-style Prawn Curry

1 liter (4 cups) chicken stock or 2 chicken stock cubes in 1
   liter (4 cups) boiling water
$4^1/_2$ tablespoons Yellow Curry Paste (see below)
250 g (9 oz) fresh medium prawns (about 12), peeled
   with tails intact, deveined
150 g (1 cup) fresh or canned bamboo shoots, sliced
2 teaspoons sugar
3 tablespoons fish sauce
2 tablespoons tamarind juice (page 7)

Yellow Curry Paste
2 stalks lemongrass, thick bottom part only, tough outer
   leaves discarded, sliced
5 cm (2 in) galangal root
2 cloves garlic
4 to 5 shallots
2 dried red chillies, soaked in warm water for 10 minutes
   to soften, deseeded and sliced
2 tablespoons turmeric powder

1 To make the Yellow Curry Paste, grind the lemongrass
and galangal root in a mortar or blender until fine. Add
the garlic, shallots, dried chillies and turmeric powder
and grind further to make a smooth, moist paste. This
paste can be stored in an airtight container in the fridge
for a month or in the freezer for 3 months.
2 Bring the chicken stock to a boil in a stockpot over high
heat. Stir in the Yellow Curry Paste and mix well. Reduce
heat to medium and simmer for 6 to 8 minutes. Add the
prawns and bamboo shoots and cook until the prawns
turn pink, 2 to 3 minutes. Season with the sugar, fish
sauce and tamarind juice. Mix well before removing from
heat. Serve with steamed rice.

Serves 4
Preparation time: **30 mins**
Cooking time: **15 mins**

Sarong Prawns (Goong Sarong)

80 g (3 oz) dried rice vermicelli (*beehoon* or *mifen*)
16 fresh medium prawns (about 300 g/10 oz)
2 teaspoons crushed coriander roots and stems
2 cloves garlic, minced
$^1/_2$ teaspoon freshly ground black pepper
100 g ($^1/_2$ cup) flour
2 eggs
1 teaspoon salt
Oil for deep-frying
Thai or Chinese plum sauce, for dipping

1 Soak the rice vermicelli in warm water for 5 to 10 minutes until soft. Drain and set aside.
2 Peel and devein the prawns, leaving the tails intact.
3 Mix the coriander roots, garlic and black pepper together. Rub the mixture onto the prawns.
4 Beat the flour and eggs together to make a batter. Add salt and mix well. Dip the prawns in the batter to coat thoroughly.
5 Divide the rice vermicelli into 16 portions. Arrange each portion in a straight line on a cotton towel and wrap each prawn individually.
6 Heat the oil in a wok over high heat until very hot and gently lower the prawns into the oil, a few at a time, making sure that the rice vermicelli sticks to the prawns. Deep-fry for 2 to 3 minutes each until golden brown and crispy. Remove and drain on paper towels.
7 Serve with plum sauce or sweet Thai chili sauce.

Serves 4
Preparation time: **30 mins**
Cooking time: **5 to 10 mins**

Pan-fried Fish with Ginger Sauce

Oil for deep-frying
3 tablespoons finely shredded ginger
500 g (1 lb) fish fillets
5 tablespoons flour, mixed
with a pinch of salt and
white pepper

Ginger Sauce
1 tablespoon oil
1 tablespoon minced garlic
250 ml (1 cup) chicken
stock or 1/2 chicken stock
cube in 250 ml (1 cup)
boiling water
2 tablespoons grated ginger
2 tablespoons tamarind juice
(page 7)
1 tablespoon oyster sauce

1 tablespoon fish sauce
2 tablespoons sugar
$^1/_2$ teaspoon white pepper

Serves 4
Preparation time: **30 mins**
Cooking time: **15 mins**

1 To make the Ginger Sauce, heat the oil in a wok over high heat. Stir-fry the garlic for about 1 minute until fragrant. Add the rest of the ingredients, stir well and bring to a boil. Reduce heat to medium and simmer for about 3 minutes until the sauce is thickened. Set aside.

2 Deep-fry the shredded ginger in 3 tablespoons of oil over high heat until golden brown and crispy. Set aside.

3 Lightly coat the fish fillets with the seasoned flour. Heat the oil in a wok over high heat and deep-fry the fillets until golden brown and crispy, 3 to 5 minutes. Place on a serving platter.

4 Pour the Ginger Sauce over the deep-fried fillets. Garnish with crispy fried ginger on top and serve hot with steamed rice.

Thai Style Steamed Seabass

1 small seabass (about 450 g/1 lb)
250 ml (1 cup) chicken stock or $1/2$ chicken stock cube in 250 ml (1 cup) boiling water
2 tablespoons sliced garlic
2 bird's-eye chillies, sliced
1 tablespoon freshly squeezed lime juice
2 tablespoons fish sauce
2 tablespoons tamarind juice (page 7)
1 teaspoon sugar
Pinch of salt
2 spring onions, thinly sliced, to serve
3 slices lime, to serve

1 Scale, clean and debone the fish.

2 Pour 3 tablespoons of the chicken stock over the fish. Place in a heatproof dish and steam until tender, about 10 minutes.

3 To make the sauce, combine the remaining chicken stock, garlic, chillies, lime juice, fish sauce, tamarind juice, sugar and salt in a wok or saucepan and bring to a boil over high heat. Reduce heat to medium and simmer for 1 to 2 minutes until the sauce is thickened. It should taste sour, sweet and salty.

4 Pour the sauce over the steamed fish and garnish with spring onions and slices of lime. Serve immediately with steamed rice.

Serves 4
Preparation time: **15 mins**
Cooking time: **15 mins**

Grilled Beef with Green Curry Sauce

500 g (1 lb) beef tender-
  loin or lean steak
1 teaspoon salt
1/2 teaspoon white pepper
375 ml (1 1/2 cups) thick
  coconut milk
2 tablespoons shaved palm
  sugar
4 tablespoons Green Curry
  Paste (see below)
1 tablespoon fish sauce

Green Curry Paste
2 tablespoons dried
  shrimp paste
1 tablespoon fresh green
  peppercorns or 1/2 tablespoon black peppecorns
1 tablespoon grated kaffir
  lime peel
2 coriander roots and stems
1 stalk lemongrass, thick
  bottom part only, outer
  leaves discarded, sliced
2 cm (1 in) galangal root
5 cloves garlic
3 to 4 shallots
2 to 3 green bird's-eye
  chillies

1 To make the Green Curry Paste, roast the shrimp paste over low flame using tongs or aluminium foil (page 7). Set aside. Grind the peppercorns, lime peel, coriander roots, lemongrass and galangal root in a blender or spice grinder until fine. Add the garlic, shallots, chillies and roasted shrimp paste, and grind further to make a smooth paste. This makes about 375 g (1 1/2 cups) of paste. The paste can be stored in the fridge for 1 month or in the freezer for up to about 3 months.

2 Rub the salt and pepper onto the beef. Grill on a char-coal or pan grill over medium heat for 5 to 10 minutes until browned on the outside but still pink and moist inside. Set aside. When cool, cut the beef into slices and arrange on a serving platter.

3 Combine the coconut milk, palm sugar and Green Curry Paste in a wok or saucepan and simmer over low heat, stirring constantly, until the sauce is thickened. Add the fish sauce and mix well before removing from heat.

4 Pour the curry sauce over the beef slices and serve with steamed rice.

Serves 4
Preparation time: **30 mins**
Cooking time: **30 mins**

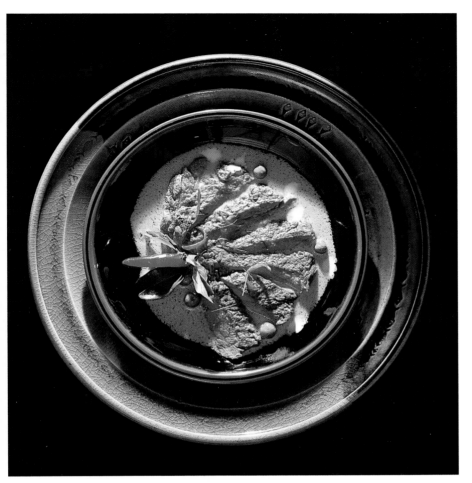

Grill the beef until browned on the outside.

Grind the peppercorns, lime peel, coriander roots, lemongrass and galangal until smooth.

Beef with Red Curry and Vegetables

185 ml ($^3/_4$ cup) thick
  coconut milk
2 tablespoons Red Curry
  Paste (page 46)
500 g (1 lb) beef tender-
  loin, sliced
125 g (1$^1/_2$ cups) eggplant,
  cut into bite-sized chunks
1$^1/_2$ tablespoons fresh
  green peppercorns or
  $^1/_2$ tablespoon black
  peppercorns
100 g (1 cup) green beans,
  sliced diagonally
4 tablespoons fish sauce
3 teaspoons sugar
80 ml ($^1/_3$ cup) chicken
  stock or $^1/_4$ chicken stock
  cube in 80 ml ($^1/_3$ cup)
  boiling water

8 kaffir lime leaves, torn
  into large pieces
Few sprigs basil leaves,
  to garnish
2 red chillies, sliced,
  to garnish

Serves 4
Preparation time: **20 mins**
Cooking time: **25 mins**

1 Heat the thick coconut milk in a wok or skillet over medium heat for about 2 minutes. Stir in the Red Curry Paste and simmer until the mixture has thickened and reduced to one-third, about 10 minutes.
2 Add the beef and stir-fry until cooked. Add the eggplant, peppercorns and green beans. Stir-fry for another minute until the vegetables are tender, then season with the fish sauce, sugar, chicken stock and lime leaves. Mix well before removing from heat.
3 Serve hot, garnished with basil leaves and chillies.

Grilled Beef with Hot Basil and Chilli Sauce

500 g (1 lb) beef rib-eye
  or lean flank steak
125 ml ($^1/_2$ cup) Hot Basil
  and Chilli Sauce (page 48)
20 g ($^1/_2$ cup) Crispy Fried
  Basil Leaves (page 38),
  to serve

Marinade
2 tablespoons soy sauce
1 tablespoon fish sauce
1 teaspoon sugar
1 teaspoon freshly ground
  black pepper

1 First make the Marinade by combining the soy sauce, fish sauce, sugar and black pepper in a bowl. Mix well until the sugar is dissolved. Pour the Marinade over the beef and marinate for about 1 hour.

2 Grill the beef on a charcoal or pan grill until browned on the outside but still pink and moist on the inside. This should take 5 to 10 minutes. Set aside to cool.

3 Cut the beef into thin slices and place on a serving platter. Pour the Hot Basil and Chilli Sauce over and serve with Crispy Fried Basil Leaves.

Serves 4
Preparation time: **1 hour**
Cooking time: **10 mins**

Minced Pork in Preserved Cabbage

300 g (10 oz) preserved
  mustard cabbage (*mui
  choy* or *mei cai*)
3 tablespoons oil
2 cloves garlic, minced
2 teaspoons crushed
  coriander roots and stems
3 shallots, sliced
250 g (9 oz) ground pork

2 tablespoons minced
  galangal or ginger
$2^1/_2$ tablespoons ground
  roasted peanuts
2 tablespoons shaved palm
  sugar or dark brown sugar
2 tablespoons fish sauce
$^1/_2$ teaspoon freshly ground
  black pepper

1 Soak the preserved mustard cabbage in cold water for about 1 hour to remove the salt. Drain and set aside.
2 Heat 2 tablespoons oil in a wok over high heat and stir-fry the garlic, coriander roots and shallots until fragrant, about 1 minute. Add the pork and stir-fry until cooked. Add the galangal root and peanuts. Mix well and season with the palm sugar, fish sauce and black pepper. Stir-fry for a further minute until the sauce is thick. Set aside.
3 In the same wok, heat 1 tablespoon oil over medium heat. Stir-fry the preserved mustard cabbage leaves for about 1 minute. Remove and set aside to cool.
4 Wet your hands. Shape the pork mixture into small balls and wrap in preserved mustard cabbage leaves.

Serves 4
Preparation time: **1 hour**
Cooking time: **20 mins**

Drain the soaked preserved mustard cabbage leaves in a strainer.

Stir-fry the preserved mustard cabbage leaves.

Shape the cooked pork mixture into small balls with your hands.

Wrap the pork mixture in the preserved mustard cabbage leaves and serve.

Steamed Coconut Custard in a Pumpkin

1 small pumpkin
  (about 500 g/1 lb)
5 eggs
90 g ($^1/_2$ cup) shaved palm
  sugar or dark brown sugar
$^1/_2$ teaspoon salt
125 ml ($^1/_2$ cup) thick
  coconut milk

Serves 4
Preparation time: 20 mins
Cooking time: 30 mins

1 Carefully cut out a 5-cm (2-in) section around the stem of the pumpkin and lift it out to form the "lid". Scoop out the seeds.
2 Lightly beat the eggs in a mixing bowl. Add the palm sugar, salt and coconut milk, and stir until the sugar is dissolved and the mixture is well blended.
3 Pour the mixture into the pumpkin. Replace the "lid" and steam the whole pumpkin in a steamer for 20 to 30 minutes over high heat, until the custard is set. Remove and set aside to cool.
4 Slice the pumpkin into wedges and serve warm or chilled.

Diced Water Chestnut in Sweet Coconut Milk

8 fresh water chestnuts,
  peeled and diced
2 drops red food coloring
50 g (¹/₂ cup) tapioca flour
90 g (¹/₂ cup) young
  coconut meat, sliced
Crushed ice

Sweet Coconut Milk
100 g (¹/₂ cup) sugar
180 ml (³/₄ cup) water
180 ml (³/₄ cup) thick
  coconut milk

Serves 4
Preparation time: 30 mins
Cooking time: 20 mins

1 To make the Sweet Coconut Milk, boil the sugar and water in a saucepan over high heat, stirring constantly until the sugar is completely dissolved. Remove and set aside to cool, then add the coconut milk and mix well.

2 Place the water chestnut dice in a bowl and sprinkle with the red food coloring, creating light and dark red spots that resemble "rubies". Soak the red water chestnut dice in 500 ml (2 cups) of water for 1 hour. Remove and drain. Roll the red water chestnut dice in tapioca flour to coat thoroughly, then place in a seive and shake off excess flour.

3 Bring a pot of water to a boil. Drop the coated water chestnut dice into the pot, stirring gently to separate, and simmer 2 to 3 minutes until they float to the surface. Remove and steep in cold water for 1 to 2 minutes. Drain and set aside.

4 To serve, place 2 tablespoons water chestnut dice in a small dessert cup. Pour over 4 tablespoons Sweet Coconut Milk and sprinkle some young coconut meat and crushed ice on top.

Index